Designs for the UNITED STATES CAPITOL
Library of Congress

Pomegranate

SAN FRANCISCO

Pomegranate Communications, Inc.
Box 808022, Petaluma CA 94975
800 227 1428; www.pomegranate.com

Pomegranate Europe Ltd.
Unit 1, Heathcote Business Centre, Hurlbutt Road
Warwick, Warwickshire CV34 6TD, UK
[+44] 0 1926 430111; sales@pomeurope.co.uk

ISBN 978-0-7649-3978-5
Pomegranate Catalog No. AA360

Pomegranate publishes books of postcards on a wide range of subjects.
Please contact the publisher for more information.

Cover designed by Lora Santiago
Printed in Korea
16 15 14 13 12 11 10 09 08 07   10 9 8 7 6 5 4 3 2 1

To facilitate detachment of the postcards from this book, fold each card along its perforation line before tearing.

American architecture can be said to have begun with the United States Capitol, conceived as early as 1791 and completed in 1865. Designed to serve a revolutionary new form of government, it was the first example of an entirely new building type. Furthermore, like the Declaration of Independence, the Constitution, and the Bill of Rights, the Capitol served as a tangible expression of the ideas of the founding fathers. The chambers necessary to the functions of the executive, judicial, and legislative branches of the new government determined the plan of the Capitol, and the two houses of the legislature established its symmetry and symbolized the balance of powers. Envisioned as the "first temple dedicated to the sovereignty of the People," its central and uniting feature was a great domed rotunda originally styled "the Hall of the People."

The drawings reproduced in this book of postcards provide clear evidence of the talent, imagination, and skill of the architects and draftsmen who participated in the creation of the Capitol—including Stephen Hallet (1755–1825), William Thornton (1759–1828), Benjamin Henry

Latrobe (1764–1820), Charles Bulfinch (1763–1844), Alexander Jackson Davis (1803–1892), and Thomas Ustick Walter (1804–1887). Housed in the Center for Architecture, Design, and Engineering (established in 2002), the drawings constitute but an introduction to the wealth of documentation on the Capitol to be found in this and related collections in the world's largest library. Architectural images are also available online via the Prints and Photographs catalog of the Library of Congress at http://www.loc.gov/rr/print/catalog.html.

C. Ford Peatross, Curator
Architecture, Design, and Engineering Collections
Prints and Photographs Division
Library of Congress

TO THOMAS JEFFERSON ESQ.
B. LATROBE. 1805.

Designs for the UNITED STATES CAPITOL

Benjamin Henry Latrobe: US Capitol. As proposed to be completed by
Benjamin Henry Latrobe. Architectural drawing showing a perspective
view of the East and North Fronts. Dedicated "To Thomas Jefferson,
Pres. U.S." Graphite, ink, and watercolor on paper, 1806. Architecture,
Design, and Engineering Collections, Prints and Photographs Division.
LC-USZC4-1090

BOX 808022   PETALUMA   CA 94975

Pomegranate

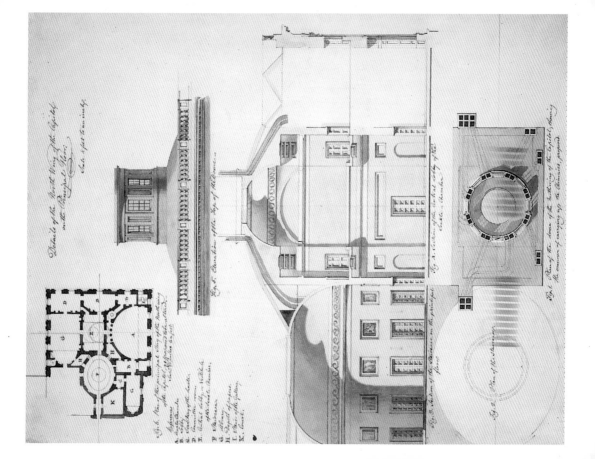

Designs for the UNITED STATES CAPITOL

Benjamin Henry Latrobe: US Capitol, North Wing. Principal Story,
Upper Stairhall (left), and Central Lobby or Vestibule (with Lantern).
Architectural drawing showing plans, sections, and elevations.
Graphite, ink, and watercolor on paper, 1807. Architecture, Design,
and Engineering Collections, Prints and Photographs Division.
LC-USZC4-122

BOX 808022   PETALUMA   CA 94975

Pomegranate

Designs for the UNITED STATES CAPITOL

William Thornton: US Capitol, East Front. Architectural drawing, rendered elevation. Graphite, ink, and watercolor, c. 1796. Architecture, Design, and Engineering Collections, Prints and Photographs Division. LC-USZC4-1097

BOX 808022   PETALUMA   CA 94975

Pomegranate

Designs for the UNITED STATES CAPITOL

Benjamin Henry Latrobe: US Capitol, President's Chair, Senate.
Architectural drawing showing elevations, plans, and details.
Ink, wash, graphite, and watercolor, 1809. Architecture, Design, and
Engineering Collections, Prints and Photographs Division.
LC-USZC4-222

BOX 808022   PETALUMA   CA 94975

Pomegranate

Designs for the UNITED STATES CAPITOL

Benjamin Henry Latrobe: US Capitol, South Wing. Hall of
Representatives. Architectural drawing, longitudinal section. Graphite,
ink, and watercolor on paper, 1804–1805. Architecture, Design, and
Engineering Collections, Prints and Photographs Division.

LC-USZC4-1244

BOX 808022   PETALUMA   CA 94975

Pomegranate

Designs for the UNITED STATES CAPITOL

Stephen Hallet: US Capitol, Proposed Scheme "D," East Front.
Architectural drawing, elevation. Ink, graphite, and watercolor,
1793. Architecture, Design, and Engineering Collections, Prints and
Photographs Division.

LC-USZC4-7191

BOX 808022   PETALUMA   CA 94975

Pomegranate

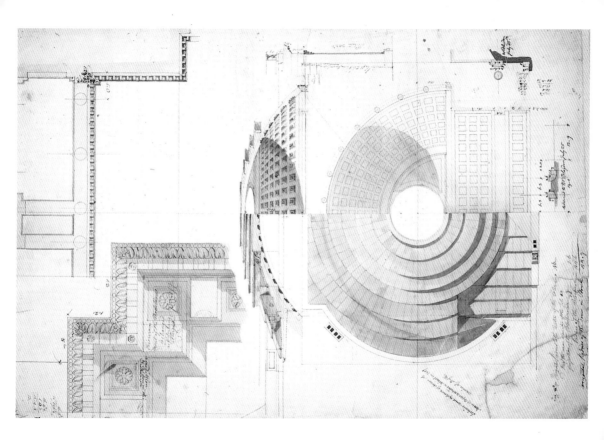

Designs for the UNITED STATES CAPITOL

Benjamin Henry Latrobe: US Capitol, South Wing. House of Representatives, Dome, Interior and Exterior. Architectural drawing showing plan, section, and details. Graphite, ink, and watercolor, 1815. Architecture, Design, and Engineering Collections, Prints and Photographs Division.

LC-USZC4-1243

CA 94975

PETALUMA

BOX 808022

Pomegranate

Designs for the UNITED STATES CAPITOL

Stephen Hallet: US Capitol, Proposed Scheme "B," East Front.
Architectural drawing, rendered elevation. Graphite, ink, and
watercolor wash, 1791. Architecture, Design, and Engineering
Collections, Prints and Photographs Division.
LC-USZC4-221

BOX 808022 PETALUMA CA 94975

Pomegranate

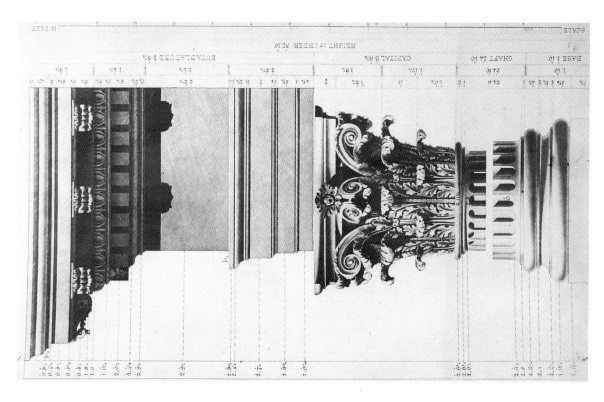

Designs for the UNITED STATES CAPITOL

Thomas Ustick Walter: US Capitol Extension. Corinthian order
capitals and entablature used on exterior. Architectural drawing,
elevation. Salted paper photograph, after 1854. Architecture, Design,
and Engineering Collections, Prints and Photographs Division.
LC-USZC4-2665

BOX 808022 PETALUMA CA 94975

Pomegranate

This section, is a mere answer to the question of the President as
to the propriety of a Doric colonnade.—

A Apis of the Vest of the House   B Speakers closet
C Speakers Gallery   D Common Gallery
E Floor of the House of Reps   F Walls of the Galleries
G Vestibule of the House   H to the Water table of floor
I Oping to rooms over the Doorkeepers, explaining of
  first over the Well drawing room of the Members

Sketch of a Section of the South Wing of the Capitol of the United States at Washington, of the Doric Order,

for the consideration of the President. U.S.

B Henry Latrobe, ———
Surveyor of the Public Buildings

Designs for the UNITED STATES CAPITOL

Benjamin Henry Latrobe: US Capitol, South Wing. Hall of Representatives and Vestibule. Architectural drawing, transverse section. Graphite, ink, and watercolor, 1804. Architecture, Design, and Engineering Collections, Prints and Photographs Division. LC-USZC4-1098

BOX 808022 PETALUMA CA 94975

Pomegranate

Designs for the UNITED STATES CAPITOL

Benjamin Henry Latrobe: US Capitol, South Wing. House of
Representatives. Architectural drawing showing elevation of
colonnade with Car of History and section of the cornice mold-
ing. Graphite, ink, and watercolor, 1815. Architecture, Design, and
Engineering Collections, Prints and Photographs Division.
LC-USZC4-1250

CA 94975

PETALUMA

BOX 808022

Pomegranate

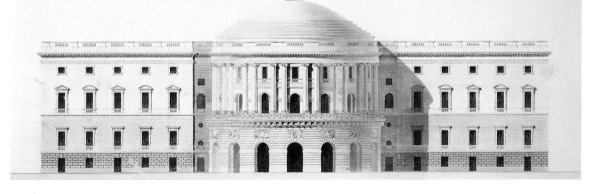

Designs for the UNITED STATES CAPITOL

Stephen Hallet: US Capitol, Proposed Scheme "E," West Front
with Conference Room. Architectural drawing, rendered elevation. Graphite, ink, and watercolor, 1793. Architecture, Design, and
Engineering Collections, Prints and Photographs Division.
LC-USZC4-1255

BOX 808022   PETALUMA   CA 94975

Pomegranate

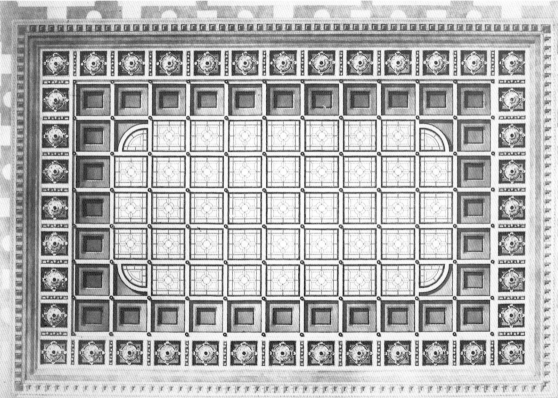

Designs for the UNITED STATES CAPITOL

Thomas Ustick Walter: US Capitol Extension. Ceiling. Architectural
drawing showing the reflected plan for the Hall of Representatives.
Salted paper photograph, after 1856. Architecture, Design, and
Engineering Collections, Prints and Photographs Division.
LC-USZC4-2662

BOX 808022 PETALUMA CA 94975

Pomegranate

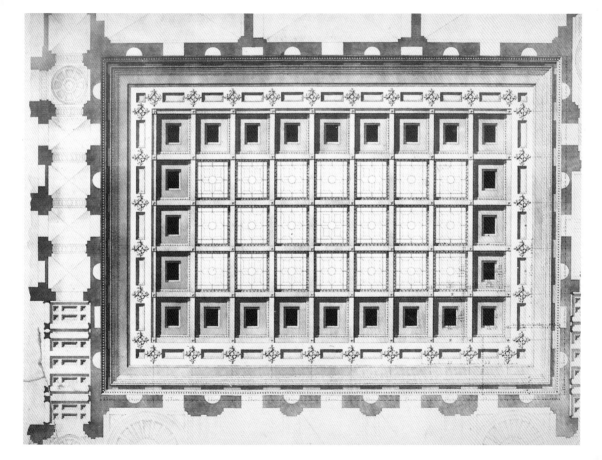

Designs for the UNITED STATES CAPITOL

Thomas Ustick Walter: US Capitol Extension, North Wing. Senate
Chamber. Architectural drawing showing the reflected plan of the
ceiling. Salted paper photograph, after 1855. Architecture, Design, and
Engineering Collections, Prints and Photographs Division.
LC-USZC4-2661

BOX 808022   PETALUMA   CA 94975

Pomegranate

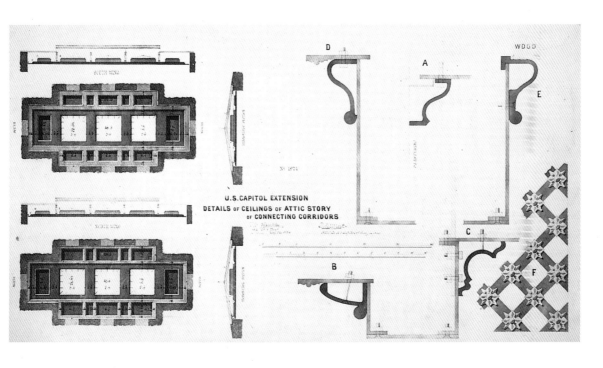

U.S. CAPITOL EXTENSION
DETAILS OF CEILINGS OF ATTIC STORY
OF CONNECTING CORRIDORS

Designs for the UNITED STATES CAPITOL

Thomas Ustick Walter: US Capitol Extension. Connecting corridors.
Attic story ceiling. Architectural drawing showing reflected plans,
sections, and details. Salted paper photograph, after 1860.
Architecture, Design, and Engineering Collections, Prints and
Photographs Division.
LC-USZC4-2664

ELEVATION OF DOME OF U.S. CAPITOL

Designs for the UNITED STATES CAPITOL

Thomas Ustick Walter: US Capitol, East Front. Dome and Portico.
Architectural drawing no. 1902, elevation. Salted paper photograph,
after 1859. Architecture, Design, and Engineering Collections, Prints
and Photographs Division.
LC-USZ62-4701

BOX 808022   PETALUMA   CA 94975

Pomegranate

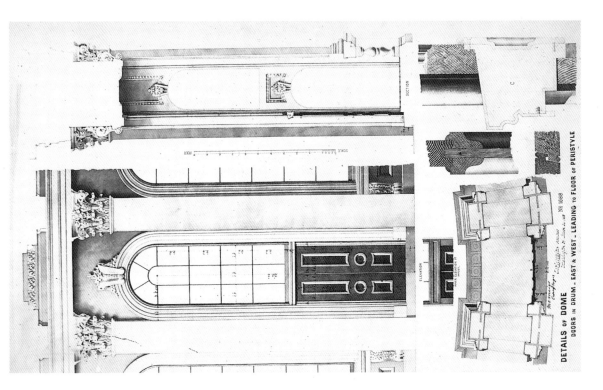

DETAILS of DOME

DOORS in DRUM - EAST & WEST - LEADING to FLOOR of PERISTYLE

N.º 1088

Designs for the UNITED STATES CAPITOL

Thomas Ustick Walter: US Capitol. Dome, Peristyle Doors.
Architectural drawing no. 1688, details, including plan, sections,
and elevations. Salted paper photograph, after 1859. Architecture,
Design, and Engineering Collections, Prints and Photographs Division.
LC-USz62-88878

CA 94975 PETALUMA BOX 808022

Pomegranate

Designs for the UNITED STATES CAPITOL

William Thornton: US Capitol, West Front with High Domed
Centerpiece. Architectural perspective sketch. Ink and wash, c.
1796.Architecture, Design, and Engineering Collections, Prints and
Photographs Division.
LC-USZC4-278

CA 94975

PETALUMA

BOX 808022

Pomegranate

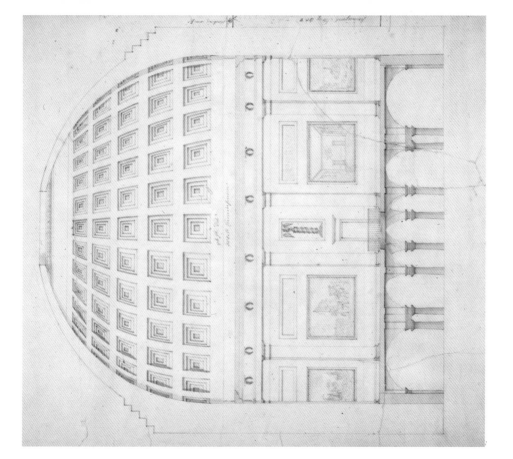

Designs for the UNITED STATES CAPITOL

Thomas Ustick Walter: US Capitol Extension, South Wing, West Front.
Architectural drawing no. XXI, elevation. Salted paper photograph,
1850s. Architecture, Design, and Engineering Collections, Prints and
Photographs Division.
ADE-UNIT 2895, no. 17 (A size)

BOX 808022   PETALUMA   CA 94975

Pomegranate

Basement Plan of Capitol

Measured and drawn by Alex J. Davis during the summer of 1832

The copper plate was divided into 18 by 21 inches square

Designs for the UNITED STATES CAPITOL

Alexander Jackson Davis: US Capitol. Basement story. Architectural drawing showing site plan and plan with two post offices, private land claims office, architect's office, and other rooms. Graphite, ink, and watercolor, 1832. Architecture, Design, and Engineering Collections, Prints and Photographs Division.
LC-USZC4-250

BOX 808022 PETALUMA CA 94975

Pomegranate

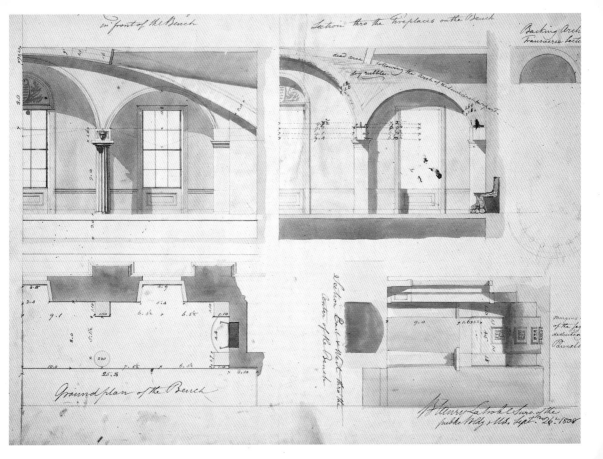

in front of the Bench

Section thro the Fireplaces on the Bench

Backing Arch
transverse Section

Ground plan of the Bench

Section East to West thro the center of the Bench

B Henry Latrobe Surv.r of the
public Bldg.s & U.S. Sept.r 26.th 1808

Designs for the UNITED STATES CAPITOL

Benjamin Henry Latrobe: US Capitol, North Wing and Court Room.
Architectural drawing, plan, and sections. Ink and watercolor,
1808. Architecture, Design, and Engineering Collections, Prints and
Photographs Division.
LC-USZC4-124

BOX 808022   PETALUMA   CA 94975

Pomegranate

Designs for the UNITED STATES CAPITOL

Thomas Ustick Walter: US Capitol. Library of Congress. Architectural drawing showing interior perspective of the new cast-iron room for the Library of Congress. Ink and watercolor, 1852. Architecture, Design, and Engineering Collections, Prints and Photographs Division. LC-USZC4-3777

BOX 808022   PETALUMA   CA 94975

Pomegranate

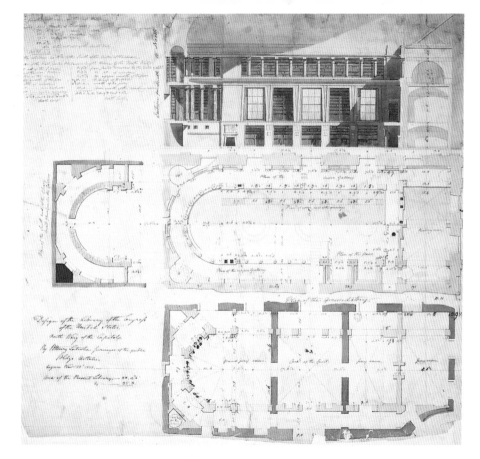

Designs for the UNITED STATES CAPITOL

Benjamin Henry Latrobe: US Capitol, North Wing. Library of
Congress. Architectural drawing, longitudinal section and plans,
showing Egyptian Revival design. Graphite, ink, and watercolor,
1808. Architecture, Design, and Engineering Collections, Prints and
Photographs Division.
LC-USZC4-226

BOX 808022 PETALUMA CA 94975

Pomegranate

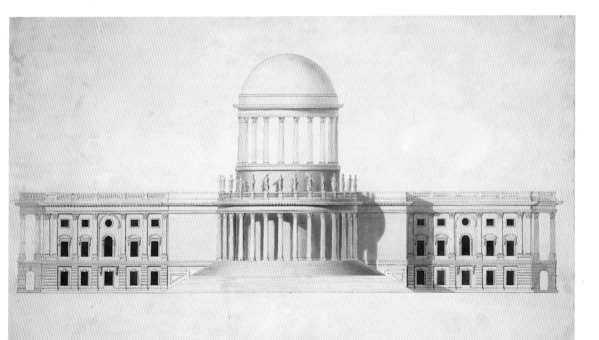

Designs for the UNITED STATES CAPITOL

William Thornton: US Capitol, West Front with High Dome.
Architectural drawing, rendered elevation. Graphite, ink, and
watercolor, c. 1796. Architecture, Design, and Engineering Collections,
Prints and Photographs Division.
LC-USZC4-113

BOX 808022   PETALUMA   CA 94975

Pomegranate

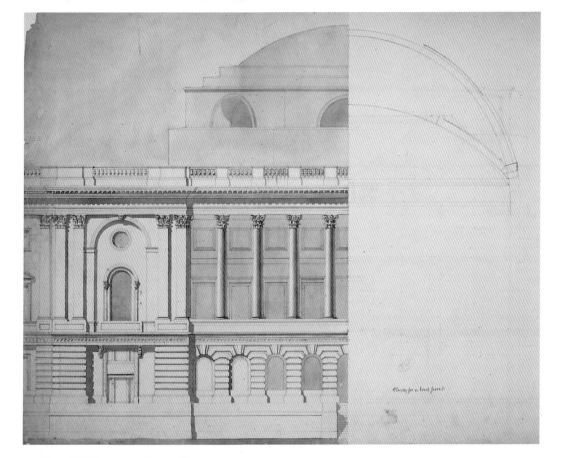

Study for a bank facade

Designs for the UNITED STATES CAPITOL

Benjamin Henry Latrobe: US Capitol, West Front. Architectural drawing, half elevation, showing a Corinthian colonnade and thermae or lunette windows under dome. Ink and watercolor, 1808–1809. Architecture, Design, and Engineering Collections, Prints and Photographs Division.
LC-USZC4-217

BOX 808022   PETALUMA   CA 94975

Pomegranate

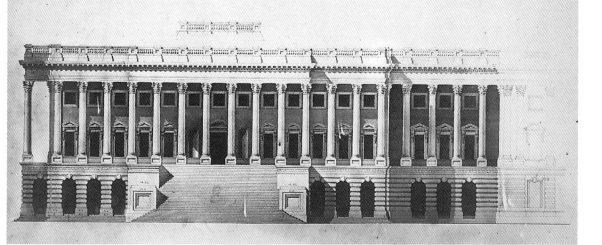

Designs for the UNITED STATES CAPITOL

Thomas Ustick Walter: US Capitol Extension, South Wing, East
Front. Architectural drawing, elevation. Salted paper photograph,
1851. Architecture, Design, and Engineering Collections, Prints and
Photographs Division.
LC-USZC4-2663

BOX 808022   PETALUMA   CA 94975

Pomegranate

Designs for the UNITED STATES CAPITOL

Benjamin Henry Latrobe: US Capitol, North Wing. Senate Chamber.
Architectural drawing, plan, elevations, section, and details showing the columns in the gallery of the entrance with capitals based
on the flower of the American magnolia tree. Ink and watercolor,
1809. Architecture, Design, and Engineering Collections, Prints and
Photographs Division.
LC-USZC4-223

BOX 808022   PETALUMA   CA 94975

Pomegranate

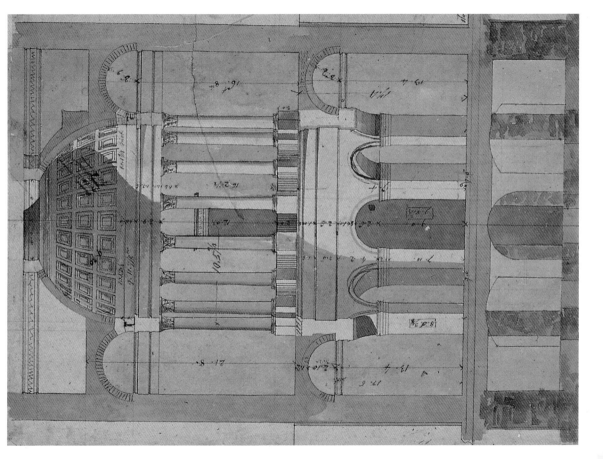

Designs for the UNITED STATES CAPITOL

Benjamin Henry Latrobe: US Capitol, North Wing. Elliptical Vestibule,
Arcade, and Colonnade. Architectural drawing, transverse section.
Graphite, ink, and watercolor, 1816. Architecture, Design, and
Engineering Collections, Prints and Photographs Division.
LC-USZC4-229

BOX 808022 PETALUMA CA 94975

Pomegranate

Designs for the UNITED STATES CAPITOL

Benjamin Henry Latrobe: US Capitol, West Front with Propylaeum.
Architectural drawing, rendered elevation. Graphite, ink, and watercolor, 1811. Architecture, Design, and Engineering Collections, Prints
and Photographs Division.
LC-USZC4-276

BOX 808022   PETALUMA   CA 94975

Pomegranate